Torn Pages

Text by Ellen Law
Illustrated by Cindy Siems

DeForest Press
of Elk River, Minnesota

DeForest Press
P.O. Box 154
Elk River, Minnesota 55330
U.S.A.
(612) 441-2363

This book is dedicated to Victor Siems, who encouraged us to tell the special stories of our families.

The red leather cover felt the agony as the pages were torn from his binding. He gasped as he helplessly watched them flutter down and scatter across the floor of the den. None of the pages knew how this horror happened, but as they lay strewn about the room the pages discussed their plight.

"Oh, I had such wonderful visions," sighed a very damp page. This page, torn from the binding, had landed in a puddle under a rubber tree plant. The small clay pot the plant grew in had overflowed during watering earlier that day. "I often heard the lady of the house talking about writing on us," lamented the page. "Now look, if she put a pen on my face, she'd tear me to shreds."

"Well, that's not what has me wrinkled with worry, "wailed a disheartened page that had fallen quite separate from the others. "Look at those logs starting to burn in the fireplace. Before we fell, I watched the lady arranging the logs and light a match to start them on fire. While we were laying open, still attached to the red cover on the desk, the phone rang and she hurried out of the den. She has been gone a long time and those flames really frighten me. Look how I'm just leaning on the edge of the hearth."

"Don't be discouraged, my friends," encouraged the red leather cover. He still lay near the edge of the large maple desk where the lady had left him open for reading. "Even though we have become separated, we are all still here. We have to believe we will all be together again. " In his efforts to inspire the pages he nearly tumbled over the edge of the desk, but managed to remain steadfast.

"How can you sound so confident?" asked a torn page, part of itself still attached to the binding of the red leather cover.

"You come from strong fibers!" explained the red leather cover. " Don't you remember the stories you told me about when you were in the North Woods? You were a giant northern white pine that stood in the center of the forest, boughs and branches above most of the other trees. Remember the stories about the stands of spruce and evergreens? Grumblers all, they were constantly whining about their lot in life. It's a wonder they weren't all mangled and broken where they stood. They always pushed and shoved one another to catch an extra ray of sun."

"It's hard to imagine, but you said that they didn't even like the cardinals and doves nesting in their branches, because the birds weighed them down and slowed their growth."

"As I listened to your tales of the North Woods, I was bewildered. Everything made those trees unhappy. Imagine, they felt the lovely snows of winter bend their limbs and the warm summer sun scorch their needles."

"You often told me how you wished you could have uprooted yourself to get away from all their grumbling. As I recall, you tried to tell them about all the good they did. You reminded them how their needled boughs sheltered all the forest animals from the snow and rain. You even tried to make them see that the birds needed their pine cone seeds for food. But, instead of listening, they complained all the more."

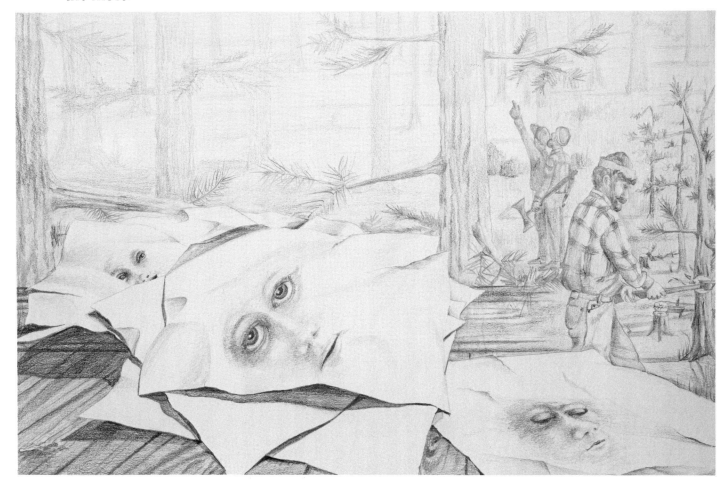

"Oh, I remember the forest," said a muffled voice coming from a pile of overlapping pages. "I recall a cool autumn day when woodsmen came walking through our grove. They wore red and black plaid shirts and carried saws and axes over their shoulders. As they walked, they talked a long time about which trees would make the best logs for burning in their fireplaces. When they stopped and stood in front of our tree, one of the men commented that ours was the most majestic he had ever seen. He said that we were destined to become something special, not just fire wood.”

"That's right.” Stated the red leather cover. “When those men walked to the group of complaining trees and chopped several of them down, you said how relieved you were to have the chance to continue your life in the forest. Yet, you recalled you were curious about the special purpose the woodsman mentioned.”

"My, that sure seems like a long time ago,” spoke up a solitary page laying near the corner of a well-worn sofa. “I was so overjoyed for those trees. They would

soon have the important job of keeping the woodsmen's homes warm and full of light during the cold dark nights of winter.” Then, he paused and started to cry, "Now, oh my, just look at us. We are nearly fuel for a fire ourselves. Is there no one around who can save us?”

"I feel lucky," stated the page in the puddle, attempting to sound unafraid. "Being as wet as I am, I doubt I will catch fire."

As the pages continued conversing with one another, the door to the den cracked open just far enough to allow the lady's brown and orange striped cat to return to the den. The cat sat for a moment, surveying the pages as they lay scattered about the room. Seemingly satisfied that nothing had changed since his last visit, the cat stretched and yawned. The glowing fire in the hearth caught his eye. As he scampered across the den to his plaid pillow that lay close to the hearth, his claws ripped and tore some of the pages. Several loose pages slid beneath the sofa, while others were pushed under the chair. Apparently, unaware of the clutter, the cat pounced up on the pillow, curled up and promptly fell asleep.

A woeful wail came from beneath the overstuffed chair that sat in front of the fireplace. Put at an angle to capture the glow and warmth of the fire, the chair was one of the coziest places in the room. And yet the page felt only the cool darkness of the chairs' shadow. "What is to become of me?" wept the page. "I am so frightened. It is dark under here and I can't see any of you. Please, one of you say something so I won't feel so alone."

The red leather cover quickly offered comfort. "Don't be afraid. I can see a corner of you peeking out from under the chair. Laying here on the edge of the desk, I can see nearly every one of you." Since he was the only part of the book still intact, he tried to give his friends a sense of hope. "I see by the mantle clock that it is nearly three, the time the lady of the house often brings her grandchildren in here for a story." By encouraging the pages the red leather cover bolstered his own faith that help would soon arrive.

"Oh, good heavens! Grandchildren! Story time! Please say it is not true!" moaned a page that was creased and torn by the cat's claws. "When they come, they always run around and play hide and seek. They will destroy all of us. We are finished!"

As he spoke the door swung completely open. The breeze from the motion lifted many of the loose pages off the floor. As if weightless, these pages were moved around the den. One of them slid closer to the stack of logs near the fireplace. Others drifted across the floor coming to rest in a jumbled heap beside some book shelves.

The lady came through the door alone. She carried a steaming cup of tea in one hand and a thick book tucked under her arm. As she entered the den, something caught her attention. Her precious pages were scattered everywhere. Tears filled her eyes.

Heart broken, she walked across the room and sat her cup of tea and book on the fireplace mantle. She crouched to pick up the pages closest to the fireplace. She then got down on her hands and knees and crawled around the room, gathering pages as she went. With great care she smoothed out pages that were torn, wrinkled or creased.

The pages seemed to nestle as the lady placed them in a pile. They began to whisper with excitement, "Can you believe it? We're nearly all together again!"

Continuing to crawl around the room, the lady looked under the footstool, sofa and lamp stand. Coming to the chair by the hearth, she reached under and pulled out the lonely page. When she was satisfied she had not missed a single page, she stood up and walked over to the page laying in the puddle of water. With the gentleness of a mother caring for an injured child, she carefully picked up the damp page and carried it to the desk. Moving the red leather cover back from the edge of the desk, she placed the wet page on the desk ink blotter. With her white cotton handkerchief, she painstakingly dabbed and smoothed out the wet page so it could dry without a wrinkle.

After a few moments, she picked up her reading glasses from the desk and put them on. Pulling out the desk chair, she sat down and began to study each page.

"This is my story!" she said aloud as she thoughtfully picked up the pages.

She talked to the pages as she would to close friends. "I have been working so many months writing! You are full of special memories. You hold the story of a family . . . my family!" As she studied each page she arranged them as they were before torn from the red leather cover. How grateful she was that even though the pages had been torn, creased and clawed, the stories were still there.

She started reading through the first chapter. Those pages were filled with stories about her father's farm equipment store. She had written about how, during the winter months, the local farmers would gather around the old pot-belly stove that warmed the parts department. While they sat waiting for their tractors to be repaired they would swap local news and interesting tales. She had included the stories she loved the most, about birthing lambs and bailing hay.

The remaining chapters contained the family's favorite songs, recipes and a variety of pictures. Each helped bring the stories to life. The songs were ones her family enjoyed singing while her mother or grandmother played the piano. The recipes were for casseroles her aunts made for holidays, birthdays and other special occasions. Some of the pages had pictures of grandma's quilts made from bits of cloth that had been thriftily saved. Also written were stories that told where the cloth scraps came from and how the quilts were lovingly sewn together to become the fabric history of her family.

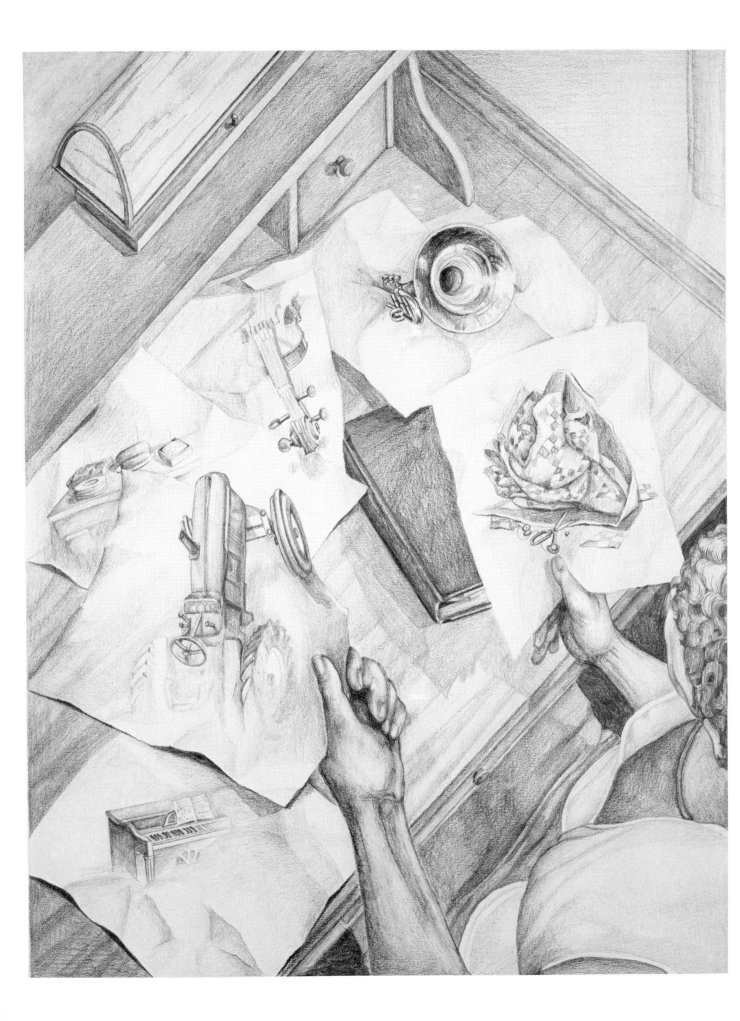

The lady sat back in the chair, pushed up her glasses and rubbed her eyes. She started talking aloud again to the pages as if they were actually listening. "A story that always makes me chuckle is about how all the cousins had to learn to play a musical instrument. The squeaking and squawking from the beginning violinists was barely tolerable. Then there were those awful sounds as the trombone almost slid into a note. The harsh off-key blare of the trumpet. Terrible! Never did sound like music!" The lady grinned. "Can you imagine, we cousins performed an annual concert for all the relatives?"

"I can still see the aunts and uncles sitting, hands folded tightly in their laps, smiles on their faces, patiently listening to that racket for nearly an hour. As I think back, I wonder if they came with cotton in their ears?"

Several more times she looked over the pages and caressed each, making sure that all the tears were mended and that every page was accounted for. When she was sure not a word had been lost, she smiled.

At last she put all the pages inside the red leather cover, placing the damp page at the top to make sure it would continue to dry flat. Carefully, she picked up the book and walked across the room to the book shelves. With one hand she moved several of the standing books to make a place to set the red leather covered book.

"To think you were nearly destroyed," she spoke lovingly to the pages. "I don't think I could bear the thought of losing all the precious pictures and memories."

"Most important, you are to be a gift to my children and grandchildren. Tomorrow, I will take you and have your binding repaired. When you are rebound, your reunion will be complete."

After one last look at the book, she gave it a loving pat, walked over and picked up the cat, and left the den. As she went through the door she reached behind her and pulled it shut tight.

The pages heard the latch on the door click. Only then did they begin to relax. The weight of the familiar red leather cover made them feel secure.

"You heard what the lady said." The red leather cover's voice was loud and full of pride. "We are important!"

He was so excited that he was almost bursting at his edges. "I'm so proud of all of you. We had some rough moments and some nearly catastrophic events."

"And," spoke up the damp page, feeling much stronger now that he was back with his friends and safe within the red leather cover, "the lady said we are covered with wonderful words and beautiful pictures. Our words tell cherished stories." He paused, and then continued in an even more powerful voice, "Imagine, the prophesy of the woodsmen has come true. We are a magnificent gift, a legacy to her children and grandchildren."

There was silence for several minutes, then the red leather cover gave all the pages a tight squeeze. "We have the most important job there is. We hold the words of the past that will be read in the future and perhaps. . . forever."

Just like the lady in this story, every family remembers special events, places and

things. We have left these pages for some of your favorite memories and pictures…

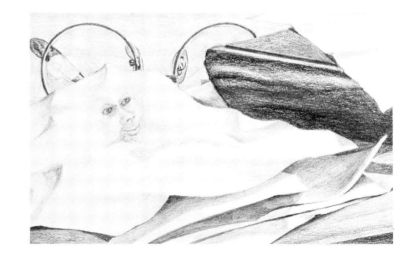